How the World's First Cities Began

Also by Arthur S. Gregor
Charles Darwin

Arthur S. Gregor

How the World's First Cities Began

Illustrated by W. T. Mars

E. P. Dutton & Co., Inc. — New York

For a dear friend
Joyce Mann

The author wishes to express his appreciation
to Dr. Andree Sjoberg of the University of Texas
for her kindness in checking the manuscript for this book.

Contents

Were you to travel in a space ship and look down at the nightside of the earth you might be able to see the lights of thousands of cities. But there was a time long ago when all you could have seen was one great dark shadow hung in the sky. . . .

I

The Life of the Hunter

A long time ago there were no cities any place on earth. There were no towns, no villages, no farms, no roads. The world was one great unending wilderness.

In those far-off days people lived in family bands. They hunted and fished and gathered roots, berries, and wild fruits. They spent most of their time looking for food. If they were lucky, they feasted. But once the feast was over, the search began all over again. Everyone in the band—fathers, mothers, and children had to work at collecting and preparing food.

Whatever the hunting folk caught or gathered they usually ate at once. Often there wasn't anything left over. Families sometimes went hungry; little children cried; old people wandered away to die in the wilderness. Life was very hard for most people.

A hunting band was generally quite small. Perhaps no more

than twenty-five men, women, and children lived together. A larger group might not have been able to find enough food for everyone.

At the present time our planet is crowded with almost three billion people. But in the days of the hunting folk, there were no more people on the entire earth than you would find in one good-sized city today. A man could walk for many days and never meet another human being. The world must have seemed a very frightening place, full of mystery and danger.

Man lived as a hunter and gatherer for perhaps a million years. Only about fifteen thousand years ago did he begin to change his way of living.

The change probably first took place in southwest Asia when a number of hunting bands started to settle down. The people in these bands stayed in the neighborhood of the same

hunting camp for long periods. In this way they came to know the surrounding countryside thoroughly. They knew just where they could find the best roots, berries, and nuts. They knew just when the plants they liked the most would be ripening.

Now it happens that in this part of the world there are places where wheat and barley grow wild. The hunting folk gathered these grains just as they gathered other wild plants that they used for food. They had no idea that it was possible for them to grow wheat and barley.

How did they find out? We really don't know. All this took place long before men kept written records. But we can imagine a way it could have happened.

A young girl may have been in the hills above her camp, gathering wild wheat for her family. We can see her cutting down the grain and then carefully carrying it all the way back to camp. But just as she gets to her hut, she trips and spills it all. Of course she tries her best to pick up every precious grain. But she must have missed some because, months later, a little patch of wheat has sprung up right next to her door.

Did everybody in the band then try the experiment of spilling a few grains next to his hut and wait around for his patch to come up? We cannot say.

But however it happened, food growing was a great discovery. People did not have to spend their lives in an everlasting search for food. They could stay in one place and plant their seed and harvest their crops.

Getting food no longer had to be a matter of guesswork or luck. People could now take control over their food supply.

They could be farmers.

If you had lived in one of the first farming villages, you would have known all the people—the grownups as well as the children. Everyone would have been your neighbor. In your whole life you might never have seen a single stranger. Your village was your world.

II

The Way of the Farmer

Once hunting folk were certain they would have a good crop every year, they probably made their camp their home. In place of huts they built sturdy houses. They became farmers and their camp became a village.

We should not think that they gave up hunting and gathering overnight. For many years they remained both farmers and hunters. The men went off into the wilderness to hunt and fish while the women stayed at home and worked in the fields hoeing and digging.

In those places in southwest Asia where the hunting people had come upon wild wheat and barley there lived wild goats, sheep, pigs, and cattle—all animals that could be tamed and raised for food.

Men who had been out hunting may have returned to their village one day with several live baby goats in tow. Before man became a farmer, these animals would have been killed and eaten right away. But now, with wheat and barley growing in the fields, there was other food at home. Instead of killing the goats, the farming people may have put them in a pen and allowed their children to take care of them. In time the goats grew up and had babies of their own.

Here was another great discovery: Man no longer had to hunt animals—he could raise them. Just as a few grains could become a field of grain, so could a few animals become a herd of animals. Man could have milk, butter, cheese, and meat, just as he had wheat and barley. And all without going outside his own little village!

A farmer rarely went far from home. Another village might be less than a day's walk away and yet the chances were he would never visit it. In a whole lifetime he might never see a single stranger. Between these early villages there was little trade. Each village was a world in itself in which people found almost everything they needed for living.

If a farmer needed a new house, he built it with the mud and reeds he took from the banks of a nearby river. If he needed clothing, he made it out of the skins of animals he had

stone he had dug up. He used materials that came from his own neighborhood and he relied on himself and his family caught or raised. If he needed a tool, he chipped it from a for the work that had to be done.

The wife of the farmer wove baskets, made clay pots, stitched clothing, and worked in the fields. His children cared for the farm animals and chased away the birds that tried to eat the growing grain. Every member of the family had a job to do.

Sometimes the farmer was able to raise more grain in his fields than his family could use. He stored whatever he had left over in big baskets and saved it for the next year. Cereals such as wheat and barley kept for a long time without spoiling. Even if the next year's crop failed, no one starved. Life was usually easier and safer for the farmer than it had been for the hunter and gatherer.

A farmer's family tended to be larger than a hunter's. The farmer welcomed more children. When they came, he increased the size of his farm and raised more food. More mouths to feed meant more workers to help him in the field.

Farmers probably lived longer than hunting folk, and their children must have been stronger and healthier. With the new way of life, the number of people in the world rapidly increased. At the beginning of the Age of Farming there may have been five million people in the world. Less than four thousand years later there were probably over eighty-six million.

Farm villages spread from their first beginnings in southwest Asia to the Nile Valley in Egypt, and then to India. Villages appeared in the Far East and in Europe. People lived in small settled communities, raised crops and farm animals, and had enough to eat.

We should not forget, however, that even after farming had caught on, there were still people who did not give up the old way of life. Even today, more than ten thousand years after farming began, a few people in far places of our planet continue to live by hunting, fishing, and gathering.

The Age of
Cities

ABOUT 100
MILLION PEOPLE →

← ABOUT 3,000 B.C.
BEGINNING OF CITIES

The Age of
Farming

ABOUT 5 MILLION →
PEOPLE

← ABOUT 8,000 B.C.
BEGINNING OF FARMING

Hunting and
Gathering

*The Age of Farming Set Off a Population
Explosion*

For countless ages men had been able to use only the strength of their own bodies to do their work. Suppose you had been the first man to think of letting an animal pull a plow across a field. You would have been filled with a sense of wonder. A force outside your body was doing your work for you. . . .

III

The Land Between the Rivers

In southwest Asia today, above the Persian Gulf, there is a country called Iraq. In ancient times it was known as Mesopotamia, a name that means "between the rivers." It is a good name because, although most of the land is a hot, flat desert, there are two great rivers that flow through it, the Tigris and the Euphrates.

Just above the Persian Gulf these twin rivers wander through huge tracts of swampland where wild birds and animals live and date palms grow. To anyone coming out of the blazing desert these swamps must look like a green fairyland.

Not too long after farming had been discovered, desert and mountain people settled down in this fertile land. They drained the swamps and built dikes to hold back the water. They cut down the high marsh grass and laid it crisscross over the muddy ground. Then they planted fields of barley and put up little huts made of mud and reeds.

The Land Between the Rivers

*The first swamp village was settled perhaps
7,000 years ago just above the Persian Gulf.*

Because wood was very scarce, the settlers built almost everything of reeds. Even their canoe-shaped boats were made of reeds that had been bundled together.

The soil of the swamps was very rich and the farmers often had three crops a year. Farms spread north out of the swampland and along the banks of the two rivers. Finally, when all the good land along the shoreline was taken, canals were cut into the banks of the rivers. Water flowed into the back country and barren desert became fertile land.

The welfare of the farmers depended on the canals and ditches that brought water to their land. If the water stopped flowing, the desert would return. A farmer could take care of the small ditches that passed through his land, but the care of the larger canals needed the help of the entire village.

During the yearly flood season the rivers rose. The farmers had to work together to repair the dikes that held back the rising water. During the dry time of the year they had to deepen the waterways and sink new wells.

When the call for help went out, all the men in the village had to drop whatever they were doing and quickly come together to clear a canal or build a new wall. If they failed to do so, there would soon be no water for anyone, no harvest, and no food.

The village could easily punish a farmer who did not answer the call. He might wake one morning and find that the other farmers had blocked off the channel that brought water to his fields. He had no choice but to obey.

At first a group of elders or older farmers may have given

the orders. Later a chieftain took charge of the waterways and became the village leader.

In return, perhaps, for his services, the farmers turned over to him a portion of their crop and some of their farm animals. These shares of what the farmer raised were the earliest taxes we know of, and the farmer probably enjoyed paying them as little as people today enjoy paying their taxes.

As the chief grew more powerful, he demanded higher taxes. His storehouse overflowed with wheat, barley, dates, and onions. His barn was crowded with sheep, goats, pigs, and oxen. Whenever crops failed, the farmers had to go to him and beg him for a little food or seed to tide them over until the next harvest. What the chief held in his storehouse and in his barn gave him the power of life and death over the village.

In some villages the chief was also the high priest who took charge of the religious holy days and the prayers to the gods. Disobeying the chief was as terrible as disobeying the gods. The first chief may have only been a superintendent of waterworks, but those who took his place behaved more and more like kings.

Neither the chief nor his many relatives and servants could possibly use all the food and goods piled up in his storehouse. What could he do with them? He could exchange them for other things he wanted. And what he wanted perhaps more than anything else in the world was copper.

In the past, tools and weapons had been made of stone, bone, or wood. But about the time the river villages were becoming rich and powerful an easy way was discovered of making them of copper. Because metal tools and weapons were a great improvement on those made of the old materials, copper became very valuable.

But how was the chief to get his longed-for copper? There was none in lower Mesopotamia. The copper mines were generally located in mountains far away from his village. What he did was to trade with those places where copper was found. And he paid for the precious metal with the grain and wool he had collected from his farmers.

On his little farm the farmer worked very hard to support his family and meet his heavy taxes. At first he did all his work by hand. But the time came when he got the idea that his cattle could take over some of the heaviest work. Instead of turning up the earth with a hand hoe or a digging stick, he now let his oxen drag a plow across his field. Farming was no longer such a back-breaking job.

The plow was a very simple invention. But it was also one of the most important man ever thought up. Formerly he had had only his own strength to rely on. Now, by using the strength of animals, he was making a force outside his own body work for him. The ox was the first step toward the steam engine, the gasoline motor, and the nuclear reactor.

A farmer behind a plow could take care of a much larger field than a man or woman grubbing into the soil with a digging stick or a hoe. He could grow bigger crops and feed more people than any farm worker had ever done before.

Larger fields meant that more water was needed. Old canals were widened. New canals were built. The twin rivers were connected by broad channels. From the main canals hundreds of branches led to the ditches that took the water into the farmers' fields. Lower Mesopotamia became a network of waterways. The desert turned green.

Animal power could be used in more ways than dragging a plow across a field. The oldest means of transportation was man's shoulders. But when the farmer began to raise cattle, he placed his burdens on their broad backs and let them do the carrying for him.

The next step was to hitch his cattle to sleds which could be pulled over the ground. Then, with the invention of the wheel, the sled became the first wagon. Goods could now be carried far beyond the village. The grain, wool, and dates that the village chief sent to far-off lands in exchange for copper were carried on wagons pulled by trains of oxen.

The villagers also sent goods by water. At first their little reed boats and wooden rafts were able to travel only on the rivers. But with the invention of the sail, the villagers learned to make use of the force of the wind. They sailed far out into the Persian Gulf and their trade spread over land and sea.

In ancient times Mesopotamia was not a single country but a land of many small cities—each with its own ruler, laws, army, and chief god. Had you lived then, you would have been very proud of your little city although it might have held no more than five thousand people and its boundaries gone no farther than the watered fields outside its walls. It was your country. . . .

IV

The Beginning of Cities

The villages that lined the shores of the twin rivers were often at odds with one another. Sometimes the villagers raided their neighbors' pasture land and drove off cattle. It was far easier to steal animals than to raise them. Sometimes they feuded about the amount of water they could draw from a common canal. Quarreling led to fighting.

To protect themselves the farmers threw up high thick walls about their villages. Sometimes two or more villages might unite to put up a common wall. Large villages became walled towns.

In time of war the farmers fled into town for safety. Since the towns were often built on a high clay mound, they were also a safe place when the rivers overflowed their banks and flooded the land. Little villages might tumble down, but the town was usually free from such danger.

The towns were centers for the worship of the gods. At holiday time the entire countryside flocked into town to visit the shrines and temples and take part in the religious festivals.

Within the walls lived special workers who did no farming. We remember that, in the first villages, almost everyone had to be a farmer if only because a man who did not farm did not eat. After a farmer had fed himself and his family, there was nothing left over for anyone else except his chief.

But in Mesopotamia, with the help of the rich soil and his plow, the farmer raised enough food to feed a good many people who did not work at farming. What the farmer brought to the chief's storehouse was used not only for trade but also to pay special workers such as the smiths who turned metal into tools and weapons. The coppersmith was perhaps the very first special worker who gave all of his time to a task other than farming. But soon there were others: carpenters, cloth weavers, brickmakers, potters, bakers, teachers, and gold workers.

As far back as fifty-five hundred years ago, men had already made the discoveries and inventions they needed for living successfully in cities. They used wheeled carts and sailing vessels for exchanging goods with distant places. They made tools of metal. They had large supplies of food on hand so that people could be freed from farm labor to become city workers.

In time, up and down the twin rivers, there arose no less than fifteen cities, each with its own ruler and its own laws. Each was a little country in itself, a city state whose control went no farther than the neighboring countryside. Villages without name were replaced by cities whose names are still remembered: Ur, Eridu, Larsa, Erech, Lagash, Nippur, and Kish.

The village chieftain had become the proud monarch of a little kingdom.

Plan of the city of Ur, showing the great wall surrounding the city, and location of major buildings and courtyards within.

The cities of Mesopotamia were small, and people lived close to one another. You did not have to go far to see your friends or do business. Today we write a letter or use the phone, but in those days people had to meet face to face. . . .

V

The Plan of the City

Round the city ran a great wall so wide that several chariots could race side by side on the top. Alongside the wall was a moat or ditch filled with water. Before enemy soldiers could climb the wall they had to swim the moat.

Outside the wall were wild animals, outlaws, and other dangers. But at night, after the heavy gates of the city clanged shut, a man could sleep soundly.

Many of the farm workers lived within the walls. In the morning they went out to take care of their low fields crisscrossed with canals and ditches. At nightfall they hurried back to their homes within the city.

The city was quite small in size. Since people usually went on foot, it was useful to have everything close by. A man could get from his home to the place where he worked in a few minutes. In time of danger everyone could come together quickly. A bell or drum sounded in the courtyard of the king's palace probably could be heard throughout the city.

In the heart of the city, surrounded by another high wall, were the palace of the king and the temples of the gods. Nearby were the homes of the nobility and the wealthy.

If you looked up at one of these homes from the street, all you would see would be a doorway and a blank wall. The windows were in the rear and opened on an inner courtyard.

From the street you passed into a little foyer furnished with

a drain and a jar of water for washing your feet. You then entered a paved central courtyard open to the sky. Off this courtyard were the guest rooms, the kitchen, a workroom, and the quarters for the slaves and the servants.

A flight of stairs led to a covered balcony running around the court. Here were the pleasant rooms with whitewashed walls in which the family lived. The floors were covered with rugs, cushions, and mats. There were low tables at which the members of the family sat cross-legged at mealtime. The house usually had at least twelve rooms. It was probably quite cool and comfortable even during the heat of a Mesopotamian day.

The dead sometimes shared the house with the living! When a relative died, he was often buried inside the house, usually in a narrow yard just off the guest room. Instead of being carried off to a distant cemetery where he might be forgotten, he remained in the house where he was born. In a way he continued to be a member of the family.

On the edge of the city farthest away from the temples and the palace were the jumbled together homes of the poor—miserable flat-topped huts of one or two tiny rooms. They were made of adobe or sun-dried mud brick. The material cost almost nothing because it could be easily dug up on the banks of the river that ran close to the city. Even today in Mesopotamia the poor are still making their homes of mud brick.

Between the walls of the houses ran crooked unpaved streets that often ended in blind alleys. The streets were so narrow that if you stretched out your arms you could touch the walls on either side. Because wagons could not get

through these streets, burdens had to be placed on a man's back or on a pack animal.

During the day the streets, like those of towns in the Middle East today, must have been very noisy and busy. Children ran about, housewives gossiped, peddlers cried their wares. Cattle and sheep on their way to market shoved passersby against building walls. Dogs and pigs fought for the garbage that lay piled up at corners.

With each rain the walls of the houses softened a little. Mud slid into the street and mingled with the refuse so that the street level rose. When a householder opened his door during a storm, a river of filth poured into his house. In order to keep the mess out, he raised the level of his door by adding a step. But, as time went by, the street continued to rise, and he had to add another step and still another.

Finally there was not enough headroom for him to get through the door. The only thing left to do was to tear down the entire house and rebuild it on the level of what had once been the roof.

Just as refuse was never removed, neither were the bricks of buildings that had fallen into the streets. New houses were built right over the ruins of old ones. A traveler, returning to his old neighborhood after a long absence, might be surprised to find it perched on a hill.

Because of impure drinking water there must have been a great deal of illness. Once an epidemic began, it must have spread like wildfire throughout the city, killing thousands. People probably lived only half as long as they do in western countries today, and the infant death rate must have been very high.

At the supermarket today prices are clearly marked. You either pay the set price or you don't buy at all. But in the ancient marketplace you never paid the first price asked for. You bargained. How much you paid depended in good part on how able a bargainer you were. . . .

VI

In the Marketplace

A stranger wandering through the narrow winding streets of a city in ancient Mesopotamia sooner or later came upon the marketplace.

It was probably very much like the marketplace of many cities in the Middle East today. To keep off the blazing sun, awnings were hung over the crowded stands and booths. Swarms of flies buzzed over the displays of food. Traders

spread their wares on the ground almost under the feet of the passerby. Magicians displayed their tricks, beggars whined for alms, wrestlers showed off their mighty muscles, barbers served their customers.

Everyone came to market—soldiers, priests, farmers, teachers, slaves, and strangers from far places. They came to meet their friends, to hear the latest news, to relay the latest gossip and to have fun. The market was more than a place to buy and sell.

A customer usually bought directly from the man who made the merchandise. For example, the potter who made pots usually sold them to his retail customers, using his workshop for the sale of his work. He probably lived with his family in the rear of his shop.

Since there was no coined money, grain was used as one means of exchange. Suppose you had a cow that was worth—let us say—ten measures of barley and you wanted to buy an ox that was worth twelve measures. To complete the sale, you gave the owner of the ox your cow plus two measures of grain.

Probably very few sales went off as simply as all that. The owner of the ox would begin by asking far more than he hoped to get. You, in turn, would offer far less than you expected to pay. Gradually the seller would go down and you go up until you both arrived at a fair price.

Your bargaining was no private matter. A crowd probably collected to watch and offer advice and encouragement. In the marketplace people enjoyed minding one another's business.

People went to market frequently. Since there was no way of storing perishable food, they must have bought in very small quantities—just enough to see them through the day. We may guess that the price of such food varied sharply through the day. Fresh fish might be high in the morning, but if it were not all sold by early afternoon, the price must have dropped sharply.

In the early villages each farmer had been a man of all work, supplying everything he needed through his own efforts whether it was an ax, a basket, or a pot. But in the city a man went to market for much of what he needed. City life could not go on without the marketplace.

In the early cities children grew up to do the kind of work their parents had done. If you were lucky enough to be born into the upper class, you might become a governor or a priest of the temple. But if you were born into a poor family, you would probably become a farmer, porter, ditchdigger, or general laborer just as your father had been. . . .

VII

The People in the City

Before men lived in cities there had been no kings or nobles. Almost everyone in the early villages had worked at the same job of raising food. One man was as good as another and each man was more or less his own master.

But when man began to live in the city, a great change took place. For the first time there were people who were very rich and some that were very poor. People were divided into two classes of citizens: a very small upper class of nobles and priests who ruled the land and ran the temples of the gods, and a very large lower class of farmers, laborers, craftsmen, and tradesmen. Outside these two groups were the slaves.

Since the nobles and the higher priests did no work with their own hands, they kept large staffs of servants. These included not only messengers, porters, and cooks, but also musicians, actors, and dancers.

The people of the lower class did the kind of work which, in the modern city, has been taken over largely by the machine. They carried heavy burdens on their backs; they dug ditches; they turned the potter's wheel; they wove cloth. Whether on a farm or within the city walls, the poor labored from dawn to dark for barely enough to keep alive.

Yet the life of the slave was even more difficult.

Armies of workers were needed to build temples and palaces or to repair the walls of the city. Where were so many laborers to be found?

Prisoners captured in war, instead of being put to death, could be put to work. A live slave was more useful than a dead enemy. In a world without steam engines and gasoline-driven motors, slaves were a cheap and plentiful source of power.

36

Slaves were not only enemies who had been captured in war. They were also people who had once been free citizens of the city. A man could be forced to become a slave because he had not paid a debt. When times became unbearably hard, a husband might sell his wife into slavery or a father his child.

People lived out their lives in the class into which they had been born. If your father had been a porter, you probably were doomed to spend your days carrying burdens on your back. Nor could you ever go to school; schooling was only for the children of the wealthy.

You did not protest too much. Like everyone about you, you believed that men were the servants of the gods. It was the gods that had decided that you were to be a porter and not a king or high priest. Though life was hard, you did not question the will of the gods.

In ancient Mesopotamia you might have been a riverman floating great rafts down the muddy river. Or you might have been a caravan driver guiding patient oxen over the desert to distant lands. One day you might come home with tales of what you had seen in the great world outside your city. . . .

VIII

Outside the City Walls

Outside the city walls ran the two mighty brown rivers. They flowed for over a thousand miles from the northern mountains to the Persian Gulf.

The twin rivers were the source of the water that turned the desert into green fields of ripening grain. They were also highways of trade that linked the cities of Mesopotamia with the outside world.

Down the great rivers floated huge rafts bringing gold, silver, timber, building stone, and copper to the cities of Kish, Nippur, Erech, Lagash, Larsa, Ur, and Eridu. At the end of their long voyage downstream the rivermen broke up their rafts and sold the timber for high prices. Wood for building was very scarce on the flat plains of the south.

Fleets of sailing vessels sailed down the twin rivers out into the Persian Gulf. They visited countries as far off as India,

returning home with ivory, pearls, gems, and hardwood. With a sail on its mast a ship could leave the sight of land and travel for great distances over the sea.

Goods were also brought to the cities by caravan. Patient oxen pulled heavily laden wagons over desert and swampland. In return for what they received, the cities sent wheat, barley, dates, and woolen cloth. Wherever boats or caravans stopped to trade, the merchandise of Mesopotamia was highly prized.

The most valuable material that came to the cities was not gold, pearls, or gems, but copper. Tradesmen and craftsmen needed copper; it could be used to make articles ranging from pins to statues. Soldiers could not get along without it; a stone dagger might shatter in a fight, but a metal dagger could be relied on. No army had a chance against its enemies unless it had a plentiful supply of metal swords, spearheads, and helmets on hand.

When copper was melted and a little tin was added, a new metal called bronze was produced. Tools and weapons made of bronze were tougher and longer lasting than those made of copper. And since copper and tin could be obtained only from afar, the cities had to trade.

We remember that the early villages had been able to get along by themselves with little or no contact with the outside world. The city, however, would die if its trade were cut off. Rich and powerful as the city was, it could not live without the world beyond its walls.

Mesopotamian cities were often at war. They had, however, no regular paid soldiers. If you were a male citizen, the chances were that you would be called into the army many times in the course of your life. . . .

IX

Cities at War

Great rafts floating downstream loaded with valuable cargo, and long caravan trains were tempting prizes. Often they were attacked and robbed as they passed the walls of unfriendly cities. The cities then went to war to protect their trade.

The armies of Mesopotamia were very powerful. The main body of an army was made up of heavily armed, spear-carrying soldiers who fought in a phalanx or close-order formation, with their tall shields arranged like a wall in front of them. Each soldier wore a cone-shaped copper helmet, a kilt or short skirt made of leather strips, and a long cloak.

In front of the phalanx moved the light infantry who fought with axes, daggers, and curved swords. The cavalry rode to battle in low four-wheeled wagons pulled by pairs of donkeys. The wheels of these clumsy chariots were made of two solid

pieces of wood clamped together and lined with leather tires. In each chariot were a driver and a fighting man armed with four throwing spears. Riding in his royal chariot at the head of all the troops, the king himself led the army into battle.

Battles were fierce and bloody, and thousands of soldiers were killed on both sides. When a city was captured, its walls

were torn down, its treasures taken, its storehouses and homes burned to the ground, and its men, women, and children led off to slavery. Only the ruins of what was formerly a great city were left behind.

Among the prisoners were the gods of the fallen city, whose statues were carried home in triumph by the victorious army.

As you came toward your home city in "the Land Between the Rivers," the first thing you saw in the distance, looming over all the other buildings, was the ziggurat, or temple tower. It was the home of the chief god of your city. . . .

X

Ruler of the City: the Priest-King

When a victorious king returned home from war, he went to the chief temple to thank the god of his city for his help.

People believed in many gods who were in charge of different activities. Nabu, for example, was the god of growing things; Enlil was the god of the wind and the rain; Enki was the god of the waters of the river. In addition, each city had its own special god who looked after it in time of peace and defended it against its enemies in time of war.

The gods were treated as though they were real people. As real people they had to eat, and they were, therefore, given daily meals of bread, milk, meat, wine, beer, and dates. None of the food was wasted. Actually it was all eaten by the hundreds of priests who took care of the temples of the gods.

Five thousand years ago, just as we do today, people won-

dered about nature. And just as we do, they asked questions: "What causes a man to fall ill?" or "Why should there be terrible floods one year and a lack of rain another year?" Today we turn to the scientists for the answers to such questions. In those days people turned to the temple priests.

According to the priests, illness was caused by evil spirits. With the aid of their magic powers the priests claimed they could cure a sick man by driving these spirits out of his body. If rain failed to come, they felt they had to remind the rain god that it was time for him to water the dry fields. They did this by pouring pure water into a vase filled with grain and dates.

The chief priest was the king himself. Just as the village chieftain had often been both chief and holy man, the king was both ruler and high priest. As the head of all the priests, it was only natural for the king to have the greatest magical power. He alone could meet and talk to the god of the city.

To get in touch with the god, the king lay down to sleep. Then in a dream the god appeared and gave the king directions for running the affairs of the city. Though the god was supposed to be the supreme ruler of the city, the king did just about what he pleased.

The home of the chief god was the ziggurat, a temple tower that loomed high above the other buildings of the city. It was an almost solid man-made mountain, twenty or more stories high, with a shrine on the roof that held a statue of the god.

The sloping walls of the ziggurat were dotted with little pottery jars. Three flights of outside stairs led to terrace gardens where the priests could rest on their way to the shrine on the roof.

Why did people build such huge towers which must have taken a tremendous amount of labor and expense? The legend was that long ago the people of Mesopotamia had lived among high mountains. When they settled on the flat plains between the two rivers, they built the temple tower so that their god would not feel lonesome for his former home.

Temple towers continued to be built long after the people who founded the first cities of Mesopotamia were gone. The biggest and most famous temple tower ever built was the ziggurat of Babylon which we know from the Bible as the Tower of Babel. It was finally destroyed by Alexander the Great.

Around the ziggurat and the smaller temples ran a thick wall. If an enemy ever succeeded in breaking through the city's outer defenses, the king, his priests, and soldiers could retire behind the temple walls and hold out for a long time.

They would not lack for food, for the wall enclosed not only temples but also storerooms, granaries, and barns. The storerooms were filled with oil, salted and dried fish, mats, wool, building stone, and timber. The granaries were packed with barley and wheat. The barns were crowded with sheep, goats, and oxen. An enemy that tried to starve out the king and his soldiers would have a long wait.

Just as the chief god was supposed to be the ruler of the land, he was also supposed to be the owner of the vast wealth of the temple.

47

In fact, the king was the real owner. He rented the temple farmlands to the farmers and then took a huge share of the crop for himself and his priests. On the temple grounds he ran huge workshops where his servants and slaves ground corn, tanned leather, worked copper and bronze, spun wool, and made wine and beer.

The priest-king claimed that he was only the manager for the god. Actually he was the biggest businessman and landlord of the entire city.

Once the temple had taken its share of a farmer's crops and animals, there was very little left for him and his family. The farmer always remained a very poor man. Why did he continue to work so hard for so very little?

He believed that what he was doing was for the benefit of the god. He thought that the god had given his city victory over its enemies in war. He thought that the god held back the flood waters and quieted the storms. He thought that the god had filled his fields with ripe grain and fat cattle. And when he entered the temple grounds carrying grain or leading his sheep and goats, he believed he was only returning to the god of his city what he owed him.

You probably would not have enjoyed going to school in ancient Mesopotamia. Your lessons would have been checked by a teacher known as the-man-in-charge-of-the-whip. . . .

XI

The First ABC's

How much was each farmer to give to the temple? That depended on how much land he had rented. It also depended on the amount of seed and the number of farm animals he might have borrowed from the temple.

How were the priests to keep track of so many accounts? They could not rely on their memory. Even if a priest had the best memory in the world, what would happen if he were to die?

The priest had to have a record more reliable than any man's memory. It had to be a record that could be understood not only by the man who made it, but also by any man who happened to take his place. What the temple needed was writing.

Writing began about the time the first cities were built in

Mesopotamia. It was probably invented by temple priests to help them keep their accounts straight.

The first writing looked nothing like ours. Men were writing long before the alphabet was invented. At first, writing was made up of signs that looked like pictures:

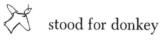 stood for donkey 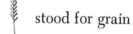 stood for grain

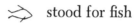 stood for fish

Later, some of the signs came to stand for spoken sounds. Our ABC's are signs that stand for sounds.

We think of writing on paper. But Mesopotamians had no paper. There was, however, plenty of clay which anyone could scoop up along the river's edge.

Clay is easy to write on. And once baked, it will last far longer than the strongest paper. We can still read letters people wrote to one another on clay five thousand years ago.

At first, the priests wrote with a sharp-pointed reed. Then they found they could write more easily with one that had a triangular-shaped tip. Instead of writing the way we do, they pressed a corner of the tip of the reed into the soft clay. Each time they pressed, they made a mark. The writing looks as though someone had dropped carpet tacks on mud.

The Mesopotamian writing system was very hard to learn, and very few people ever learned it. Hundreds of signs had to be mastered and, to make matters more difficult, many of the signs had more than one meaning. A king who could read and write was very proud of himself. A businessman usually did not take the trouble to learn to write but instead hired a scribe or writer to do his writing for him.

Very few businessmen could write their own names. And yet the law demanded that every business agreement be signed. To solve the problem, people used a round seal. This was a small stone that looked like a tiny rolling pin. Cut into the stone was a picture or design that stood for the owner's name. All he had to do when he wished to sign his name was to roll the seal over the wet clay. The imprint that came out served as his signature.

A boy who wanted to learn to read and write had to go to school. The regular schools were run by the temples. There were also private schools which were often held in the home of the principal.

The principal was called "school father," the teacher was called "big brother," and the pupil "school son." We know that school was very strict because there was also a teacher known as "the-man-in-charge-of-the-whip."

School Son began his lesson by taking a ball of wet clay and

flattening it out smoothly. Then he copied a list of words Big Brother had written out for him. When the lesson was over, he rolled up the clay and used it over again. His notebook never wore out.

We have found thousands of the clay tablets on which Mesopotamian schoolboys wrote their lessons long ago. They made as many mistakes as boys and girls do nowadays.

When a schoolboy grew up he became a temple scribe keeping accounts or making copies of tablets stored in the temple library. Sometimes he set up shop for himself in the marketplace and made out records for merchants and wrote letters for those who could not write. In the busy city there was always plenty of work for the scribe.

Today, in the Middle East, you can still see the scribe at work in the marketplace. However, instead of using a clay

tablet and a wedge-shaped reed, he now uses paper and a typewriter.

The business of temple and marketplace, and the exchange of goods with far-off places would have been almost impossible without the use of written records. The simple business of the early village could take place by word of mouth, but city living depended on writing.

In Mesopotamia the temple scribes quickly discovered that writing could be used for more than just keeping accounts. They could also record the commands of their kings, the prayers of their priests, and the deeds of their heroes.

They could store information and ideas in the temple library just as they could store wheat and barley in the granary. Writing gave them a reliable way of holding on to what they had learned and passing it on to others.

If you were in lower Mesopotamia today and standing on top of a high mound of earth in the flat yellow desert, you could see for miles in all directions. And yet you would be unable to find the great canals, the green fields, the thick walls or temple towers of the ancient cities. Where are the cities? One of them is right under you! The mound on which you stand marks all that is left of a once proud city of the Land Between the Rivers. . . .

XII

Under the Desert Hills

The city was a meeting place of strangers. At holiday time the city was filled with people who came to pray at the temples of the gods and take part in the religious parades and festivals. Travelers came to gaze at the wonders of the city. They took home with them tales of what they had seen and heard on the banks of the twin rivers. Rivermen, caravan drivers, and wandering traders carried the news of the city to far-off places.

Cities sprang up in other parts of the world. As time went by, villages became cities in Egypt, India, China, and Europe. Indians of Mexico and Central and South America built cities of their own, although they almost certainly had never heard of the cities of the Old World.

As we look back, we can understand why the first cities in the world began in Mesopotamia.

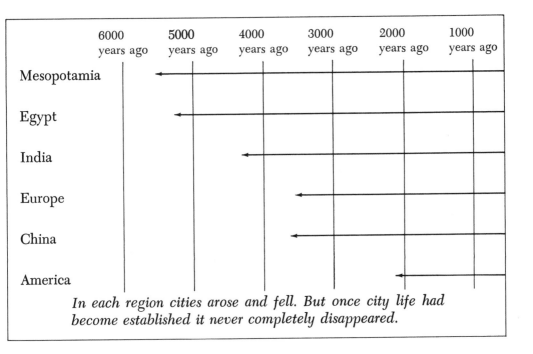

	6000 years ago	5000 years ago	4000 years ago	3000 years ago	2000 years ago	1000 years ago
Mesopotamia						
Egypt						
India						
Europe						
China						
America						

In each region cities arose and fell. But once city life had become established it never completely disappeared.

The twin rivers provided a reliable water supply. They also were highways of trade that brought goods from far-off places. Each year the rivers carried down from the northern mountains a deposit of rich soil in which crops grew easily. Large numbers of people could live close to one another and yet have enough food to eat.

The farmer raised so much food that he was able to feed not only himself and his family but also other kinds of workers. Freed from the need of producing food, these special workers had the time to learn to read and write, to use metal, and to make use of new inventions such as the wheel, the plow, and the sail.

The land on which the cities rose had once been desert. To get water to their fields, people had to learn to work together in large groups. Such training helped to get them ready for other large-scale public works such as building city walls and great temples. A city cannot exist without cooperation.

What happened to the cities of the Land Between the Rivers? What happened to the proud cities of Ur, Erech, Larsa, Lagash, Nippur, and Kish? Where are they now?

They vanished a long time ago. In some cases the rivers shifted their banks, leaving the city without water for its fields and without water for its people. The fields returned to desert, and the people moved away.

But man himself was sometimes a worse enemy than nature. Though men learned to work together within the city walls, they did not learn to live at peace with their neighbors in the outside world.

Armies, kings, and rival gods clashed in savage battle. Losing cities were set afire and their people enslaved and scattered. The victors turned homeward in noisy triumph, dragging the fallen gods behind them, only in turn to fall victims themselves to stronger foes.

Once a city was deserted its houses crumbled, its great walls fell, its temples and palaces tumbled to the ground. Canals filled with mud, wells dried up, and green fields turned brown.

Later other people came and, over the ruins of the old city, they built houses, streets, markets, and palaces. The level of the land rose, and so the new city perched on top of a high hill.

But the time came when these new cities were also gone. Clouds of sand blew across the blazing plain and covered

temple and marketplace, the poor man's hut and the rich man's home. Foxes and jackals scurried where once the hard-working farmer had turned the moist rich earth. Only the wide desert remained.

Today you can still see the two great brown rivers of Meso-potamia winding their way out of the northern mountains down to the Persian Gulf. Out of the burning desert you can see what seem to be tall flat-topped hills rising into the sky.

You and I know that they are not hills but the ruins of the very first cities men built, over five thousand years ago in the Land Between the Rivers.

Cities today grow larger and larger. They spill over their boundaries and swallow the surrounding countryside. Five thousand years ago it was a short walk from the center of the city to the city walls. Today you may have to ride an hour before you reach open country. . . .

XIII

Cities Around the World

The old cities of Mesopotamia are gone. But in their place thousands of cities now dot the entire planet. Today more people than ever live in cities. The cities take up more and more space. They reach toward each other and the countryside between them disappears. Where one city ends, another begins. We live in the age of the supercity.

Five thousand years ago most people either lived in farming villages or continued to follow the life of the hunter and gatherer. Today, on the other hand, almost one person out of every three on earth lives in towns and cities. Over one half of the people living in the United States are city dwellers.

If you will look at the chart, "The Ten Largest Cities in the World," you'll get an idea of how huge cities are nowadays. Calcutta in India is the last city on the list and yet probably more people live in Calcutta today than lived in all of the cities of the world five thousand years ago.

> ### The Ten Largest Cities in the World
>
> (The number of people, indicated at the right, includes not only those living within the city proper but also those in the thickly settled region around the city.)
>
> | | | |
> |---|---|---:|
> | 1. | New York | 14,000,000 |
> | 2. | Tokyo | 10,000,000 |
> | 3. | London | 8,000,000 |
> | 4. | Paris | 7,500,000 |
> | 5. | Buenos Aires | 7,000,000 |
> | 6. | Shanghai | 7,000,000 |
> | 7. | Los Angeles | 6,500,000 |
> | 8. | Moscow | 6,500,000 |
> | 9. | Chicago | 6,000,000 |
> | 10. | Calcutta | 4,500,000 |

From the time of the beginning of cities until a short time ago, most cities did not grow very large. In fact, many shrank in size. Some turned into towns and villages; others disappeared altogether. A little more than one hundred years ago, however, cities began to get bigger. Today, like a snowball rolling downhill, they are growing faster and faster. They are growing so fast that it will not be long before more than half the people in the world will be living in city areas.

What has caused this great shift in human affairs?

One of the important reasons has been the enormous increase in the amount of food farmers can raise. We know that in Mesopotamia men were able to live in cities because enough food came from the farm to feed them. These cities, however, remained quite small by our standards. If they were to grow larger, the farmer would have to be able to raise more food.

But the amount those early farmers could raise was limited. Just as long as they had to depend on their own muscles or those of animals, they were never going to be able to feed many people. Most people would have to continue to spend their lives as food producers.

About thirty-five hundred years ago, the secret of making tools of iron was discovered, probably by mountain people of northeastern Turkey, and the Age of Iron was born. Iron is one of the commonest metals in the earth's crust, far cheaper than copper. A farmer who could never have afforded a bronze ax could now afford one made of iron.

Iron was much stronger and more useful than bronze. With his trusty iron ax a farmer could cut down trees, break up the ground, and dig drainage canals. He could use land he never could have farmed in the past. He could raise more food and therefore feed more people.

But though the farmer had better tools he still continued to rely chiefly on his own strength and that of animals to do his work.

But the invention of a practical steam engine by James Watt less than two hundred years ago opened the way to new sources of power. Today mankind is making use of the energy found in coal, oil, gasoline, and even the atom.

The farmer, who once dug with a hoe or plowed with a pair of oxen, now does his work with tools and machinery driven by a gasoline or diesel motor. The amount of food the farmer raises has increased enormously. And more and more people have been freed to live and work in the city.

One machine can do the work of several men. As machines become more powerful, fewer farm workers are needed. In search of new work, millions of people flock to the city. All over the world, the flow from village to city continues.

As the number of people in the city increases, they require more space for living and working. The modern city swallows space. The ancient city could not spread very far because people had to get about chiefly by walking. The modern city, however, can extend for many miles because people can now depend on buses, cars, and trains for transportation. A man can live far from his job and yet get to work on time every day.

There are no walls about the modern city. The city has burst its skin and taken in surrounding communities. Farm villages disappear and suburbs take their place. You may have to travel hours for a breath of country air.

The very size of the modern city brings us problems that did not trouble the ancient city dweller. Many thousands of workers travel into the heart of the city from the outskirts every day. The buildings in which they work are so tall that the sky is almost blotted out. The streets are crowded and noisy with traffic. Automobile fumes and factory smoke often fill the air. Wastes pour into the rivers and lakes and dirty the water.

And yet people live far better lives than did city dwellers

in ancient times. In the modern industrial city man is no longer a pack animal. The machine does much of his work for him. A child no longer need do the work his father did. He can go to school and when he grows up, discover that a wide choice of jobs awaits him.

The city is perhaps man's greatest invention. Hunters and gatherers had to take the world pretty much as they found it. Almost all their time was spent in keeping out of danger and collecting enough food to keep from starving. They could not change their world. All they could hope for was to fit into it.

But the city dweller has invented a world of his own. He does not have to accept what he sees about him. If the city is not what he would like it to be, he can change it. He can turn his city into a clean, orderly, and beautiful place in which to live.

Index